Reasons Some Sellers are in Trouble

There are many types of sellers who are in financial trouble with their mortgage:

➤ Sellers who could afford their home when they bought it, but have since lost their job. They may have taken a different job but it pays much less and they realistically need to downsize.

➤ Sellers who were out of work for health or other reasons for a period of time and can pay the payments now but cannot catch up on the back payments.

➤ Sellers who could afford their home at the interest rate they started with, when they bought it, but the rate has adjusted due to an ARM and they cannot afford the higher payment with the adjusted rate.

➤ Sellers who were not completely honest regarding their income and got a "no doc" loan. They may have felt optimistic when they were approved but were not realistic and never could afford the home.

Good real estate agents develop a counseling attitude toward their clients to understand their needs and therefore be able to provide sound guidance.

Get to know your clients…what do they want? Do they want to stay in the home? Is that realistic for them? If the loan could be restructured, adding the past due amount to the end of the loan, could they afford to keep up with the monthly payments? What if the ARM could be refinanced as a 30-year fixed loan at a much more attractive rate?

Encourage sellers to talk with their lender…are they intimidated? Embarrassed? Assure them that the lender does not want their home, but only wants to find a solution. Encourage them to not give up.

Remember—every foreclosure we save is one home we don't have to sell before this market turns around.

Homeowners should take the following steps as soon as they know they will not be able to make their mortgage payment:

> Call the lender immediately to discuss loan workout solutions. The lender's/servicer's name will be on the owner's billing statement. The owner should obtain the name of the supervisor of the workout department. (may also be called the loss mitigation department.)

> Advise clients that it may take persistence and several telephone calls to reach the lender.

> If the homeowner is unable to work with the lender, they may contact a HUD approved Housing Counseling Agency by visiting www.hud.gov or calling 800-569-4287 (The HUD housing and counseling line)

> The www.efanniemae.com website has valuable information for owners. They encourage owners to know their rights.

> Remind clients that unfortunately there are foreclosure schemes in the marketplace.

> Advise clients to talk only to HUD-approved counselors.

Options include:

> **Refinance**

A new loan — with new terms, interest rates and monthly payments — that completely replaces your current mortgage. Even if your home value has decreased, you may be able to refinance your loan as part of the government's Home Affordable Refinance Program (HARP). Refinance benefits:

- Make your payment more affordable by lowering your interest rate or adjusting the terms of your loan
- No negative impact to credit score
- Stay in your home and avoid foreclosure

➢ Repayment Plan

An agreement between you and your mortgage company that lets you pay the past due amount on your mortgage payments over a specified time period in order to bring your mortgage up to date. Repayment plan benefits:

- Catch up on your past due payments over an extended period of time
- Less damaging to your credit score than a foreclosure
- Stay in your home and avoid foreclosure

➢ Forbearance

An offer by your mortgage company to temporarily suspend or reduce your monthly mortgage payments for a specified period of time. Forbearance benefits:

- Have time to improve your financial situation and get back on your feet
- Less damaging to your credit score than a foreclosure
- Stay in your home and avoid foreclosure

➢ Modification

An agreement between you and your mortgage company to change the original terms of your mortgage—such as payment amount, length of loan, etc. You may be eligible for the government's Home Affordable Modification Program (HAMP) created to help struggling homeowners. Modification benefits:

- May reduce your monthly mortgage payments to a more affordable amount
- Less damaging to your credit score than a foreclosure
- Stay in your home and avoid foreclosure

➢ Short Sale

A short sale is the sale of a home for less than the balance remaining on your mortgage. If your mortgage company agrees to a short sale, you can sell your home and pay off your mortgage balance with the proceeds. Short sale benefits:

- Eliminate or reduce your mortgage debt
- Assistance for relocation may be available
- May be able to recover your credit score—and get another mortgage—faster than if you went through foreclosure

> ### Deed-for-Lease™   (Fannie Mae only)

A new program that allows you to temporarily lease your home. You first transfer the ownership of your home to the mortgage company (called a Deed-in-Lieu of Foreclosure, see below) in exchange for release from your mortgage loan and payments. You can then rent the property back—at an affordable rate—and remain in the home as a tenant. Deed-for-Lease benefits:

- Stay in your home and neighborhood—no need to move or relocate
- May be able to recover your credit score faster than if you went through foreclosure
- Assistance for relocation may be available at the end of your lease
- Avoid foreclosure

> ### Deed-in-Lieu of Foreclosure

With a Deed-in-Lieu of Foreclosure (DIL), transfer the ownership of your property to your mortgage company in exchange for a release from your mortgage loan and payments. DIL benefits:

"*In a **short sale**, the servicer allows the borrower to list and sell the mortgaged property with the understanding that the net proceeds from the sale may be less than the total amount due on the mortgage. The short sale must be an arm's length transaction with the net sale proceeds (after deductions for reasonable and customary selling costs) being applied to a discounted ("short") mortgage payoff acceptable to the servicer. The servicer accepts the short payoff in full satisfaction of the total amount due on the first mortgage.*"

"*In a **deed-in-lieu of foreclosure (DIL)**, the borrower voluntarily transfers ownership of the mortgaged property to the servicer in full satisfaction of the total amount due on the first mortgage. The servicer's willingness to approve and accept a DIL is contingent upon the borrower's ability to provide marketable title, free and clear of mortgages, liens and encumbrances.*"

With either the HAFA short sale or DIL, the servicer may not require a cash contribution or promissory note from the borrower and must forfeit the ability to pursue a deficiency judgment

Avoid Rescue Scams

- **Help is free!** HUD-approved housing counseling agencies can help you negotiate with your lender or loan servicer. There is never a fee to get assistance or information from your mortgage company or a **HUD-approved housing counselor**. Beware of any person or organization that asks you to pay a fee in exchange for housing counseling services or modification of a delinquent loan. *Do not pay—walk away!* Call 1-888-995-HOPE (4673) for free housing counseling.
- **Beware of anyone who says they can "save" your home if you sign or transfer over the deed to your house.** Do not sign over the deed to your property to any organization or individual unless you are working directly with your mortgage company to forgive your debt.
- **Don't sign papers in exchange for a promise that someone else will pay off your mortgage.** ALWAYS be sure to read and understand all paperwork before signing to ensure that you are not unknowingly giving someone else ownership of your home.
- **Never submit your mortgage payments to anyone other than your mortgage company without your mortgage company's approval.** Scammers might ask you to make your payments to them; however, they pocket your payments instead of sending them to the lender.
- **Beware of anyone who says that you don't need a real estate professional or title company when selling your home.** You should always have a real estate professional, attorney or a title company to help you with any transaction involving your home.
- **Know the person you do business with.** Before responding to any person or organization offering to "save" you from foreclosure, find out if the organization is HUD-approved. Find a housing counselor on the HUD.gov website. Your lender or a HUD-approved housing counselor is the safest source of information and help.

When the Homeowner Cannot Keep the Home

Once the homeowner has decided that they are unable to keep the home, the next step may be a short sale. Here are some things you will need to know about the seller before deciding if you can help them:

- Who is their lender? Is their loan FHA, VA, Conventional?
- Do they have more than one lien on the property?
- They will need to get (or give you permission to obtain) the pay off figures on all loans.
- Are they current on all payments?
- What happened to cause them to get past due on their payments? (Is it a true hardship)
- Do they have a tax and insurance escrow account? If not are the taxes current?
- Do they have past due HOA dues? IRS or Mechanics liens?
- Are there any legal actions in progress? (Foreclosure, bankruptcy)
- Are they in communication with the lender? Who? What is being considered?
- Are they working with any counseling service?
- Do they have an attorney? (Name and number.)
- Will the seller cooperate in getting the short sale package together?
- Does the seller have assets? (Including retirement accounts)
- Is the seller agreeable and willing to use any of their own assets if required?
- Does the seller have a realistic opinion of market value?
- Does the seller have the patience to see this through?

Preparing the CMA

Remember the home is not worth less because it is a short sale. It may be worth less because of deferred maintenance. And certainly the seller's motivation is different on a short sale. Usually time is critical. You will need to be very competitive but reasonable with your CMA. Remember the lender will be obtaining other opinions of value. The lender will order an "as is" appraisal and is going to require a sale close to that value.

Do the CMA first as though repaired to average condition, like the comps. "Repaired value". Estimate the repairs needed (to bring it to average condition) and subtract 1-2 times the estimate from the "repaired value" to obtain an "as is value". Be sure to have photos for the lender to prove why the repairs are needed.

Doing the Seller's Net Sheet

Prepare the Seller's Net Sheet being sure to include all of the things that you learned from the seller in the initial interview. Be sure the loan amounts are "payoff figures". Include all loans, past due taxes, HOA dues, etc.

When the seller's net is a negative number, and the seller does not have the ability to come to closing with a check, the transaction will depend on the lender's approval of a short sale. The lender may consider a short sale when the borrowers situation is a result of a hardship. Buyer is either past due on their payments or delinquency is eminent.

Seller Must Make a Decision

Seller cannot be trying to modify or refinance the loan and also doing a short sale.

The decision of trying to stay in the home with the previous alternatives need to be explored first

If the seller cannot stay in the home the last two alternatives are short sale then foreclosure or deed in lieu of foreclosure

Confidentiality vs. disclosure

Article 12 National Association of REALTORS® Code of Ethics

REALTORS® shall be honest and truthful in their real estate communications and shall present a true picture in their advertising, marketing, and other representations. REALTORS® shall ensure that their status as real estate professionals is readily apparent in their advertising, marketing, and other representations, and that the recipients of all real estate communications are, or have been, notified that those communications are from a real estate professional.*(Amended 1/08*

Forms

Two forms that agents may want to include in their listing package are a Request for Mortgage Information) and a Seller's Authorization to Release and Advertise Certain Information. These forms need to authorize the agent to include remarks such as "all offers will be contingent upon seller's lender's approval" in MLS which will let other potentially interested parties know that the final decision will not lie with the seller. MLS rules require the remarks to be shown only in private remarks in MLS.

When the short sale is disclosed agents may, at their discretion, advise other agents (again, in private remarks) how any reduction in the gross commission established in the listing agreement may be affected as required by the lender as a condition of approving the sale, and will be apportioned between the listing office and selling office.

MLS rules

From the North Texas Real Estate Information System—check your MLS Rules

NTREIS SECTION 10 – Other participant compensation

10.01 The listing participant shall specify on each listing filed with the MLS the compensation offered to other participants for their services in the sale (or lease) of the listed property set forth in such listing. Such offers are unconditional except that entitlement to compensation is determined by the other participant's performance as the procuring cause of sale (or lease).

The listing participant's obligation to compensate any other participant as the procuring cause of sale (or lease) may be excused if it is determined through arbitration that, through no fault of the listing participant and in the exercise of good faith and reasonable care, it was impossible or financially unfeasible for the listing participant to collect a commission pursuant to the listing agreement.

In such instances, entitlement to cooperative compensation offered through the MLS would be a question to be determined by an arbitration hearing panel based on all relevant facts and circumstances including, but not limited to,

- why it was impossible or financially unfeasible for the listing participant to collect some or all of the commission established in the listing agreement;
- at what point in the transaction did the listing participant know (or should have known) that some or all of the commission established in the listing agreement might not be paid;
- and how promptly had the listing participant communicated to other participants that the commission established in the listing agreement might not be paid.

The above rules are taken from the NTREIS MLS system. Your local MLS may have different rules or obligations regarding participant compensation in a similar transaction. Please be sure to refer and be familiar with your local MLS rules regarding this subject.

Now For the Good News

On February 24, 2009 Fannie Mae issued a directive to their servicers to stop renegotiating the commission (unless the total exceeds 6%) in the process of refusing or accepting a short sale. Recently HUD and Freddie Mac have issued a similar directive to their servicers. Since that will affect conventional loans owned by Fannie Mae and Freddie Mac and FHA loans the hope is that the practice will spread to all loans.

A Little History

When the number of foreclosures began to accelerate a few years ago lender began to try to find ways to minimize their losses. The government began to create programs to attempt to help. One such program was the Home Affordable Modification program (HAMP) in 2009.

Home Affordable Modification Program (HAMP-created in 2009)

Conventional loans owned by Fannie Mae or Freddie Mac may be modified into a 15-30 year fixed rate mortgage. The following is required:

- Existing loan was created before 2009.
- Current payments exceed 31% of monthly gross monthly income
- Property is owner occupied and 1-4 family.
- Homeowner has experienced a financial hardship and is at risk of default.
- Homeowners have enough income to support the new payment of less than 31% of gross monthly income
- If you're *not* unemployed, but you're still struggling to make your mortgage payments, you may be eligible for the **Home Affordable Modification Program (HAMP)**. HAMP can lower your monthly mortgage payment to 31 percent of your verified monthly gross (pre-tax) income, which can provide savings of hundreds of dollars per month.
- Borrowers ask their lender for the **Request for Modification and Affidavit (RMA).** The **RMA** starts the process.

More History......

- Lenders sent thousands of letters to at risk homeowners inviting them to apply for modification under HAMP
- Many homeowners applied
- Some were successful at modifying. Many applied to modify but were not successful and never closed.
- **Foreclosure were still growing.....**
-

In 2010 the Home Affordable Foreclosure Alternative Program (HAFA) was born

- Lenders needed an alternative to foreclosures
- Nothing was standardized
- NAR encouraged the US Treasury to help
- US Treasury developed HAFA in 2009 and it was effective in April 2010
- FNMA and FHLMC developed their own program based on HAFA (with differences) effective August 2010
- FHA and VA do not participate in HAFA, but have their own programs

Home Affordable Foreclosure Alternatives (HAFA)

- If you can't afford your mortgage payment and it's time for you to transition to more affordable housing, the Home Affordable Foreclosure Alternatives (HAFA) program is designed for you.
- <u>Two options for transitioning out of your mortgage:</u>
- 1. <u>A short sale</u>. In a short sale, the mortgage company lets you sell your house for an amount that falls "short" of the amount you still owe.
- 2. <u>A Deed in Lieu of Foreclosure</u>. In a DIL, the mortgage company lets you give the title back, transferring ownership back to them.

HAFA Changes Things

- The borrower submits a **Request for Approval of a Short Sale (RASS)**
- The lender determines a borrower's eligibility and issue the **Short Sale Approval (SSA). (pre-approval)**
- If a purchase agreement is received before the borrower has sent the RASS an **Alt.RASS** will be sent with the purchase package.
- Lender is to approve or deny a short sale purchase agreement within 10 days. If the purchase agreement meets the pre-approved terms, it must be approved.
- The seller <u>must</u> be released from all future liability on the 1st loan and subordinate liens. No Deficiency judgments. No notes to sign.
- Foreclosure sale is suspended once the SSA is sent to the borrower.
- Mortgage payments are reduced to an affordable level or not required.
- The seller may receive relocation expenses at close of escrow.
- Servicers receive incentives to process the short sale or Deed In Lieu.
- Subordinate lien holders may receive up to $6000 total aggregate for payoff of subordinate liens. There is no 6% cap per lien on the Treasury program. (Fannie and Freddie have a 6% of the unpaid principal balance cap per subordinate lien holder up to an aggregate total of $6000.)

HAFA Advantages for Sellers

- If a short sale is not successful, a deed-in-lieu of foreclosure may be possible. Seller may receive relocation assistance
- (<u>On Fannie Mae Loans only</u>) may be able to lease the home back at below market rent . (Fannie Mae Deed-for Lease).

Is a Short sale better than a Foreclosure?

- May be better than a foreclosure on the seller's credit report.
- The seller may be able to negotiate how it will be reported to the Credit Bureau with the lender.
- A foreclosure can decrease their credit score as much as 200 points and stays on their report for 7 years.
- Better than having one more vacant property.

   Vacancies=deterioration, vandalism, theft, etc.

Definitions

- **Borrower**: the homeowner/seller who makes payments on the mortgage loan.
- **Servicer**: the company to which the borrower makes payments. The servicer is the entity that processes all paperwork and approves or denies the HAFA short sale or DIL, consistent with the rules of the HAFA program and their written policy as filed with the US Treasury.
- **Investor:** the owner of the mortgage loan. In some cases loans are serviced by the investor, but in most cases the investor is a third party
- **SSA: Short Sale Agreement**. The agreement outlines the roles and responsibilities of the servicer and borrower and provides key marketing terms, including list price or acceptable sales proceeds and the approvable closing costs. If the borrower submits an executed sales contract to the servicer consistent with all the conditions of the SSA, the servicer should approve the short sale.
- **RASS: Request for Approval of Short Sale.** The document that the borrower submits to the servicer to request approval of a short sale contract based on a previously issued SSA. The borrower must attach a copy of the executed sales contract and all addenda
- **Alt. RASS: Alternative Request for Approval of Short Sale.** The document the borrower submits to the servicer to obtain approval of a

short sale contract entered into between a buyer and seller prior to an SSA having been issued.

- **DIL: Deed-in-Lieu of Foreclosure.** The process of deeding the home to the lender instead of going through a foreclosure.
- **MANP: Minimum Acceptable Net Proceeds.** The minimum amount the servicer will accept in a short sale. Also known as **Acceptable Sale Proceeds**.
- **MI: Mortgage Insurer.** The company that issued mortgage insurance on the borrower's loan. Note: There can be mortgage insurance on the first mortgage with the monthly MI premium paid by the borrower. On the second, the loss protection coverage premium is normally a one-time fee paid by the lender.

A Little More History

- The hope was that many of the people that applied for **HAMP** and already had applications on file (but had not been able to modify) would be easily approved for a short sale under **HAFA.**
- Since the lender already had the application(including the **RMA**) from the borrower on file they could get the short sale preapproved, then instruct the borrower to hire a real estate agent and market the property

If the Borrower applied to modify their loan under HAMP the lender already has the RMA.

- Borrowers that have previously applied to modify their loans under the HAMP program will have completed a RMA (Request for Modification and Affidavit). It is a form that allows the lender to determine the buyers eligibility for **HAMP** or **HAFA**. The **RMA** includes financial and hardship information. The **RMA** is needed when beginning a short sale.
- **What if the Borrower never applied for HAMP?**

If the borrower has not been in the **HAMP** program previously, and ask about a short sale, most lenders will require the Request **for Modification and Affidavit (RMA)** to be completed first. Even though the Borrower does not plan to modify their loan now the lender needs the information that form provides so it will probably be required.

It is important to use the forms supplied by the specific loan servicer as they each have slight differences.

Borrowers that have previously applied to modify their loans under the HAMP program will have completed a RMA (Request for Modification and Affidavit). It is a form that allows the lender to determine the buyers eligibility for HAMP or HAFA. The RMA includes financial and hardship information. The RMA is needed when beginning a short sale.

The Perfect HAFA

1) The lender sends the borrower the forms to submit the package including the **RMA.**

2) The Borrower submits the package.

3) The Servicer has 30 days to approve or deny.

4) If approved the Servicer sends the Borrower the **SSA (Short Sale Agreement)** and the **RASS (Request for Approval of Short Sale)** The **SSA** includes a list price or a Minimum **Net** Proceeds Amount. (MANP)

5) Now the property must be listed with an agent.

6) The SSA must be returned to the servicer within 14 days along with a copy of the listing agreement and information about other liens. Borrower keeps RASS until a contract is being sent

7) Marketing for up to 120 days (can be extended)

8) When a contract is received and accepted by the buyer and seller it must be submitted along with the **RASS** within 3 days

9) Servicer approves or disapproves the purchase offer within 10 days.

10) Servicer cannot require closing sooner than 45 days for contract acceptance.

11) Seller receives relocation assistance and is released from all liability on all liens

Two Types of Short Sales

1. The lender forgives the debt. This is a requirement under HAFA. (This is considered debt forgiveness may be taxable income for IRS purposes; clients should check with a tax consultant.)

2. The lender requires the buyer to sign a note to repay the difference between the amount due on the mortgage and the amount they receive at the time of the sale. In this instance, the debt is not forgiven.

Seller Representation on a Short Sale

- REALTORS® who are helping homeowners negotiate a short sale owe obligations to that homeowner—who is the client.

- REALTORS® are to communicate with the lender only at the direction of the client.

- The duty of confidentiality is owed to the homeowner.

- It is important (with the homeowners permission) to contact the lender as soon as possible after taking the listing.

- Be persistent in attempting to find the decision maker at the lender's office. Ask for the Loss Mitigation Department or Loan Work Out Department.

Junior Lien Holders

- Ask the primary lien holder if they are going to be in communication with the junior lien holders or if you or the seller's attorney should contact them to negotiate the amount to satisfy them.

- Send the junior lien holder the same short sale package when submitting a contract.

What If the Seller Already Has the SSA??

- How **wonderful** if the borrower has already done a lot of the following with the lender and the lender has issued the Short Sale Agreement along with the Minimum Acceptable Net Proceeds amount.

- Now all you need to do is submit the purchase offer along with the RASS and wait for approval. ************YEA!!!

Unfortunately.......

- Most of the time (probably at least 90% of the time) you are the first point of contact with the borrower and the rest is up to you.

- In that case the sooner you start putting the package together for the lender the better.

- Some lenders will want the borrower to get the package together and submit it immediately with an RMA and some will want you to wait and send it with a purchase offer. Communicate with the Lender.

The Short Sale Package

- A knowledgeable listing agent and a cooperative seller can help the lender make the short sale run smoother.

- If the short sales has not been preapproved and the borrower does **not** have the SSA, the listing agent can save time later by having the short sale package ready to provide to lender with an offer or sooner.

- Some lenders will open the file before you receive an offer and will want you to send the documents immediately. Others want you to wait until you have a purchase offer.

- Include the complete package again with the offer.

- Each lender has their own requirements for the Short Sale Package.

- Check the Lenders web site for specific instructions.

- The following package is only a guideline.

- Many of the forms will be the same for each package and can be prepared in advance.

The package needs to include:

- A cover letter from the agent to the lender

- The lenders' Short-Sale payoff application

- The RMA

- A letter from the seller authorizing the lender to communicate with the listing agent.

- Current pay stubs showing YTD income and W2s.

- Self employed, provide a copy of the previous two year's income tax paperwork.

- Current bank statements

- Disclosure of all assets, all liabilities and all monthly expenses.

- A copy of the homeowner's credit report.

-

- Medical bills, disabilities, divorce papers, or proof of unemployment help verify the hardship.

- The Hardship Letter, in their own words and writing, containing:

  A. The current situation that will not allow the owner to pay in full

  B. Negotiation with the lender to accept less than full payment. It should include an "I'm "

  C. Statement that the "next option for them will be foreclosure".

- A CMA showing actives, pendings and solds for the last 6 months.

- Repair estimates and photos of needed repairs

- Economic data for the area. Stats, number of foreclosures, short sales in MLS.

- A complete marketing history for the property

- Copies of the purchase agreement and listing agreement. The RASS or the Alt. RASS.

- A preliminary HUD 1 based on the offer.

- A pre-approval letter for the buyer

Offer/Contract Procedures

- The sales contract is an agreement between the buyer and the seller.
- Real estate licensees are obligated to help their client negotiate the very best contract for themselves.

> The seller has the right to reject offers

>> 📄Some states have a Short Sale Addendum that can be attached when clients are involved with a short sale. If your state does not have one you may want to see an attorney to have one prepared for your use. All things marked 📄can be handled in the Addendum.

> The sale must be reported to MLS as active-contingent within three days of the effective date.

> The homeowner and the buyer sign the contract.

> The agent fills out the effective date and delivers the earnest money and option money as agreed.

>> 📄The Short Sale Addendum makes the contract contingent upon lender approval.

> The homeowner and the buyer sign the contract.

> The agent fills out the effective date and delivers the earnest money and option money as agreed. (Option money to Seller NOW and Earnest Money to Escrow Office NOW)

📄If the Buyer has a right to terminate during an option period under the Texas contract, the Short Sale Addendum says:

> A. Buyer and Seller sign the contract and get an original effective date.

> B. Earnest money and option money get delivered immediately and right to terminate begins immediately.

📄C. Nothing else is required until Seller's Lender approves the sales contract.

📄D. When Seller notifies Buyer that Lender has approved the sale the effective date is **amended** to that new date.

📄E. All other requirements of the contract including the option days begin on the **amended** effective date.

> A copy of the negotiated, signed contract along with the **RASS** will need to be submitted to the lender within 3 days.

> When you have a purchase contract before a seller is qualified for **HAFA** go to the servicer's Web site and determine if they have an **ALT. RASS** submittal package. If not, request the **Alt. RASS** package from the servicer.

Mortgage Debt Relief Act

Money forgiven by a lender on a short sale or a foreclosure can be considered taxable income. Between 2007 and 2013 some was not taxable because of the Mortgage Debt Relief Act.

The Act expired at the end of 2013. Any debt that is forgiven will probably be taxable income.

The lenders other option is to issue a judgment against the borrower for the money lost.

Always advise a client to check with their CPA and their attorney.

Multiple Offers on a Short Sale

> Submit all offers to the seller—the homeowner, who is the client—even after they have a pending contract.

> The seller has the option of negotiating a second offer as a back-up contract. Both a Back-Up Addendum and a Short Sale Addendum should be attached.

> Send a second offer to the seller's lender only at the seller's instruction.

> The seller may have agreed to tell lender about all offers.

> Submission of a second offer may nullify the progress on the first offer's acceptance. If the second offer is for more money, the seller will probably want to submit it to the lender (it may reduce the amount the seller will ultimately be asked to sign a note to pay later) and it may increase the possibility of lender approval.

Buyer Representation on a Short Sale

What if you are representing the buyer on a short sale? It is very important that your buyer client completely understand that buying a short sale will be a long process and that no one has the ability to hurry the lender. Having a good, pre-qualified buyer will help the process. Let the buyer know that the decision making will be based strictly on which of the following is better for the lender:

- Approving this transaction, or
- Going forward with the foreclosure

Ideal Buyers for a Short Sale (Educate the Buyer)

- Have no contingencies.
- Have patience (occasionally approval can take up to as much as six months. .Many transactions now are happening faster.
- Have the resources to repair after closing.
- Accept that the lender will make the final decision and cannot be rushed.
- Understand that even though the buyer and the seller have agreed to the terms of the contract the lender may not agree to the terms. Buyer and Seller may have to renegotiate to obtain lender approval.

Questions the Buyer's Agent Should Ask the Listing Agent

- Have they processed other short sales with this lender?
- Are there junior liens and are there any plans to satisfy the junior liens?
- Is the short sale package ready for submission or has it already been submitted?

What If Foreclosure has already been Initiated?

If the property has already been posted for foreclosure, there is a possibility the department handling the foreclosure will proceed to sale even though the workout department is reviewing a contract for approval. If that happens, the seller no longer owns the property and the contract is automatically terminated. The buyer must be aware of the risk.

Buyers that are on a time schedule are probably not good candidates for buying a short sale. If they are interested in a property and want to pursue it, the agent will want to be sure to use the option to terminate so that the agent can continue to show the potential buyer property and the buyer can walk away from the short sale property. If the buyer finds another property he likes, he can use his right to terminate the short sale contract. The buyer may find that he wants or needs to proceed more quickly than he originally anticipated.

Even if your short sale has been approved, if the lender goes to foreclosure sale it is over.

Short Sale Lender Approval Letters

Read Carefully. The seller may need to clarify with the lender or his/her attorney.

- Does the lender say they are releasing the security interest in the property?
- Does the lender say they are releasing or cancelling the promissory note?
- Does the lender say they are forgiving the deficiency?
- Does the letter relate how the second liens will be handled?
- Does the letter give an on or before closing date?

Why Short Sales Fail

- Incomplete short sale package
- Package not submitted per lender instructions
- Offer too low
- Buyer not strong enough
- Lender took too long and buyer backed out
- CMA did not compare to the other BPO's lender obtained
- Interior photos were not included or did not back up the buyer's offer
- The investor may be giving the lender specific instructions on how much they can discount the price from the BPO values
- The junior lien holder cannot be satisfied (try to determine what this will take prior to contract)

Test Your Knowledge

1	True or False	The Cannons of Professional Ethics, the NAR Code of Ethics and MLS rules apply to all transactions, including short sales and foreclosures.
2	True or False	MLS rules mandate that the listing broker pay the other broker the fee advertised in MLS, regardless of the ability to collect the full commission according to the listing agreement.
3	True or False	Becoming more knowledgeable about financing and different types of mortgages will help agents to prevent future foreclosures.
4	True or False	Lenders always forgive the unpaid portion of the debt on a short sale.
5	True or False	MLS rules permit the listing agent to advise buyers agents of how any reduction in the gross listing commission will be apportioned between the two offices if a short sale is being disclosed.
6	True or False	During a short sale, a listing agent has a duty of full disclosure to the lender.

7	True or False	Homeowners need to be aware that there are predators, pretending to be foreclosure rescue companies, just looking for vulnerable owners.
8	True or False	According to the Short Sale Addendum, the effective date of the contract will be amended to the date the seller notifies the buyer of the lender's approval of the sale.
9	True or False	The TREC promulgated Short Sale Addendum provides for an automatic termination for the buyer if the lender does not provide consent for the sale by a certain date.
10	True or False	Agents can help prevent foreclosures by being aware of the alternatives.
11	True or False	Once the owner has given the lender permission to communicate directly with the listing agent, it is ok for the agent to stop keeping the homeowner informed of all the details of the transaction.
12	True or False	Debt forgiveness is sometimes considered taxable income and the seller should check with her tax consultant.
13	True or False	The fiduciary duty of reasonable care includes knowledge of financing for a buyer's agent.

Answers

1	**True** or False	The Cannons of Professional Ethics, the NAR Code of Ethics and MLS rules apply to all transactions, including short sales and foreclosures.
2	True or **False**	MLS rules mandate that the listing broker pay the other broker the fee advertised in MLS, regardless of the ability to collect the full commission according to the listing agreement.
3	**True** or False	Becoming more knowledgeable about financing and different types of mortgages will help agents to prevent future foreclosures.
4	True or **False**	Lenders always forgive the unpaid portion of the debt on a short sale.
5	**True** or False	MLS rules permit the listing agent to advise buyers agents of how any reduction in the gross listing commission will be apportioned between the two offices if a short sale is being disclosed.
6	True or **False**	During a short sale, a listing agent has a duty of full disclosure to the lender.

7	**True** or False	Homeowners need to be aware that there are predators, pretending to be foreclosure rescue companies, just looking for vulnerable owners.
8	**True** or False	According to the Short Sale Addendum, the effective date of the contract will be amended to the date the seller notifies the buyer of the lender's approval of the sale.
9	**True** or False	The TREC promulgated Short Sale Addendum provides for an automatic termination for the buyer if the lender does not provide consent for the sale by a certain date.
10	**True** or False	Agents can help prevent foreclosures by being aware of the alternatives.
11	True or **False**	Once the owner has given the lender permission to communicate directly with the listing agent, it is ok for the agent to stop keeping the homeowner informed of all the details of the transaction.
12	**True** or False	Debt forgiveness is sometimes considered taxable income and the seller should check with her tax consultant.
13	**True** or False	The fiduciary duty of reasonable care includes knowledge of financing for a buyer's agent.

ABOUT THE AUTHOR

Peggy obtained her real estate sales license in 1969 and the real estate broker's license in 1971.

She has stayed connected to the real estate industry ever since. She has actively listed and sold property, managed foreclosure properties, worked in several mortgage loan servicing departments for Dallas Federal Savings and Loan, in Dallas, Texas, and in 1991 started teaching real estate classes.

Peggy presented continuing education classes for real estate brokers and salespeople as well as teaching pre-licensing classes for beginning agents. She has been a senior instructor for the Graduate REALTOR® Institute (GRI) in which she teaches legal issues, pricing property, contracts and marketing classes.

Ms. Santmyer is the author of a series of mandatory continuing education classes (MCE) that meet the educational requirements of the Texas Real Estate Commission to renew a Texas broker or salespersons license.

Peggy served as a member of the Texas Real Estate Teachers Association (TRETA) and held the Certified Real Estate Instructor (CREI) designation. She is also a member of the National, Texas and MetroTex Associations of REALTORS.® She has served on the Professional Standards Committee and the Education Committee for the Texas Association of REALTORS®

Peggy has earned and held the ABR, CREI, SRES, GRI and TAHS designations/certifications during her career.

Recently retired for teaching Peggy plans on focusing her energy on writing real estate materials. Her mission always is to assist real estate agents in the knowledge to serve their clients well.

Bibliography

Texas Real Estate License Act, as amended by the 83rd Texas Legislature, Regular Session. Effective January 1, 2014 Texas Real Estate Commission, PO Box 12188, Austin, Texas 78711-2188.

Code of Ethics and Standards of Practice of the National Association of REALTORS®, effective January 1, 2014 National Association of REALTORS®, 777 14TH Street, NW, Washington DC 20005

A Study of Residential Foreclosures in Texas prepared by the Texas Department of Housing and Community Affairs, September 29, 2006. TDHCA, PO Box 13941, Austin, Texas 78711-3941.

A press release dated October 23, 2008, ***Attorney General Abbott Calls for Mortgage Deferment Legislation To Help Struggling Homeowners.***
www.oag.state.tx.us/oagnews/release

Texas Realtor Magazine, December, 2008. www.REALTOR.org/realtormag

EXAMPLE- HAFA FORMS and LETTERS

Home Affordable Foreclosure Alternatives Program – Short Sale

A "short sale" is specifically designed to help borrowers who are unable to afford their first mortgage and want to sell their home to avoid foreclosure, even if the sale price may not pay off the amount owed on their mortgage. A short sale requires a number of parties (you, the buyer, your real estate broker, and sometimes mortgage insurance companies and other lenders) to work together to make this option successful. However, it could be a good solution for your current situation.

How Does a Short Sale Work?

Pre-Sale—we will start by approving a list price for your home or give you the acceptable sale proceeds (the minimum amount that we must receive after sales costs) from the sale of your home. We will also identify the sales costs (broker commissions and closing costs) that may be deducted from the final sales price. You then list your property (like any home sale) with a local real estate broker at the approved price.

Offer—when you get an offer on your home, you will submit the required documentation and we will approve the sale if it is in line with what we agreed to.

Closing—once the sale closes, we will release you from all responsibilities for repaying your mortgage. Plus, you will receive $3,000 to help pay some of your moving expenses. (The check will be paid to you by the settlement agent as part of the closing.) In the event there is any money left over from the sale after paying the entire amount you owe on the mortgage plus the approved sale costs, you will not be eligible to receive the $3,000.

To Participate in the Short Sale Program

Please note, there is no guarantee that your home will sell under this program, and you are responsible for determining whether you want to sell your home for the price and terms described in this letter. The following pages detail your responsibilities, additional information on the short sale process and the Terms and Conditions. **Additionally, this letter constitutes an agreement between us and you ("Agreement") so please read it carefully and completely.**

If you agree to the terms of the Agreement and want to proceed with a short sale, you must complete, sign and return the Agreement back to us. If you have questions, please contact us directly between the hours of [insert hours] at [insert toll free number.]

Sincerely,

[Servicer Name]

Attached:

Exhibit A –Short Sale Agreement

Short Sale Program—Your Responsibilities

You have until [*insert date 120 calendar days from the date of this letter*] to sell your house. After that date, this Agreement terminates, unless it is extended by us. During this time you have certain responsibilities. You must:

☐ Keep your house and your property in good condition and repair and cooperate with your broker to show it to potential buyers.

☐ [*Insert only if applicable:*] Make partial mortgage payments of $_____ by the first day of each month beginning on _____ 1, 20___ until your house is sold and title is transferred. While you are selling your house, you still legally owe the full amount of your current monthly mortgage payment. However, as part of this Agreement, we will accept this reduced payment until the house is sold and closes or this Agreement expires. These payments do not constitute a modification of your mortgage.

☐ be able to provide the buyer of your home with clear title. To start, determine if you have other loans, judgments or liens secured by your home, such as a home-equity line of credit or a second mortgage. <u>If there are such liens, you will need to either pay these loans off in full or negotiate with the lien holders to release them before the closing date. Under this program, you must make sure other lien holders will agree not to pursue other legal action related to the pay off of their lien, such as a deficiency judgment. You can get help from your broker to negotiate with the other lien holders.</u>

☐ we may allow up to 6% of the unpaid principal balance of each loan (not to exceed an aggregate of $6,000 for all the loans in total) to be paid from the sale proceeds to help get a lien release. If you have these types of liens or loans on your home, please gather any paperwork you have (such as your last statement) and send it to us when you return this signed Agreement. Remember, clearing these other liens and delivering clear and marketable title is your responsibility.

☐ at several stages of the short sale process, such as after an offer is received, you will need to complete some paperwork. You are responsible for returning all documents within the time allowed in this Agreement.

If you fulfill these responsibilities, we will postpone any foreclosure sale during the period of this Agreement.

To Accept This Offer

Please sign and return this Agreement. All owners of the property must sign this Agreement.

Obtain your broker's signature to acknowledge this Agreement, because your broker plays an important role selling your property. The Short Sale Program sections (pages 2-4) contain important information that you and your broker will need to review and discuss.

Include a copy of your signed listing agreement.

Include information on other liens secured by your home (such as home equity loans, homeowner association liens, tax liens or judgments).

[*Insert only if applicable:*] Complete and sign the Hardship Affidavit form.

We must have these documents by [*insert date 14 calendar days from this request*]. Please send us these documents at the following address: [*insert servicer address*].

You can't list the property with or sell it to anyone that you are related to or have a close personal or business relationship with. In legal language, it must be an "arm's length transaction." If you have a real estate license you can't earn a commission by listing your own property. You may not have any agreements to receive a portion of the commission or the sales price after closing. Any buyer of your property must agree to not sell the home within 90 calendar days of the date it is sold by you. You may not have any expectation that you will be able to buy or rent [*servicer may delete "or rent" in accordance with investor guidelines*] your house back after the closing. Any knowing violation of the arm's length transaction prohibition may be a violation of federal law.

We will need to talk to your broker and others involved in the sale. By signing this Agreement, you are authorizing us to communicate and share personal financial information about your mortgage, credit history, subordinate liens, and plans for relocation with your broker and other third parties that could be involved in the transaction including employees of the United States Treasury and its financial agents, Fannie Mae and Freddie Mac.

The difference between the remaining amount of principal you owe and the amount that we receive from the sale must be reported to the Internal Revenue Service (IRS) on Form 1099C, as debt forgiveness. In some cases, debt forgiveness could be taxed as income. The amount we pay you for moving expenses may also be reported as income. We suggest that you contact the IRS or your tax preparer to determine if you may have any tax liability.

We will follow standard industry practice and report to the major credit reporting agencies that your mortgage was settled for less than the full payment. We have no control over, or responsibility for the impact of this report on your credit score. To learn more about the potential impact of a short sale on your credit you may want to go to http://www.ftc.gov/bcp/edu/pubs/consumer/credit/cre24.shtm.

Deed-in-Lieu language if applicable:

If by the termination date of this Agreement, you have complied with all your responsibilities but are unable to sell your home, we will allow you to convey ownership of your home and all real property secured by your mortgage loan (your "Property"). While this action, called a deed-in-lieu of foreclosure, will not allow you to keep your Property, it will prevent you from going through a foreclosure sale and it will release you from all responsibility to repay the mortgage debt. Additionally, you will still be eligible to receive $3,000 to help with your moving expenses.

You and all other occupants must vacate your Property and provide clear and marketable title with a general warranty deed or local equivalent by [*insert date at least 30 days after the date of this Agreement*]. You must leave the house in broom clean condition, free of interior and exterior trash, debris or damage, and all personal belongings must be removed from the Property. The yard must be clean and neat and you must deliver all the keys and controls, such as garage door openers, to us. You may be required to sign standard pre-closing documents as well as attend a closing of the conveyance of your Property where all borrowers on the mortgage must be present.

You must also be able to deliver marketable title free of any other liens. We will allow up to six percent (6%) of the unpaid principal balance of each subordinate lien, in order of priority, not to exceed $6,000 in aggregate for all subordinate liens, to be deducted from the sale proceeds to pay subordinate lien holders to release their liens. We require each subordinate lien holder to release you from personal liability for the loans in order for the sale to qualify for this program, but we do not take any responsibility for ensuring that the lien holders do not seek to enforce personal liability against you. Therefore, we recommend that you take steps to satisfy yourself that the subordinate lien holders release you from personal liability.

By signing this letter, you are agreeing not only to a short sale but also to a deed-in-lieu of foreclosure if a short sale is not successful. If you have any questions about the deed-in-lieu of foreclosure, please call us before signing and returning this letter.

Short Sale Program—Receiving/Accepting an Offer

When you receive an offer on your home, within the next 3 business days, you will send us a Request to Approve a Short Sale (RASS) form, a copy of which is attached to this Agreement as Exhibit A1. You will also need to send along a copy of the signed purchase offer and evidence that the buyer has funds to purchase the home, such as a letter that the buyer is approved for a mortgage loan. Within 10 business days of our receipt of these documents, we will approve the sale if it is within the terms and conditions of this Agreement and any other liens are released.

When the sale closes in accordance with this Agreement, we will accept the net sale proceeds (all the funds that remain after the approved sales costs have been paid) in full satisfaction of your mortgage with us and will release you from all future liability.

We hope you decide to take advantage of this short sale option. If you or your broker have any questions about this Agreement please call us at [insert servicer phone number].

If you would like to speak with a counselor about this program, call the Homeowner's HOPE™ Hotline 1-888-995-HOPE (4673). The Homeowner's HOPE™ Hotline offers free HUD-certified counseling services and is available 24/7 in English and Spanish. Other languages are available by appointment.

Short Sale Agreement Terms and Conditions

List Price or Acceptable Sale Proceeds. [*Choose one and delete unnecessary text.*] [You agree to list the property in "as is" condition for [dollar amount].] OR [We will accept a sales contract where the proceeds from the sale, less the expenses stated in paragraph 5. *Allowable Costs*, nets [dollar amount].] We are not responsible for the accuracy of the list price and have no responsibility to you in the event the property is not sold. We may require you to adjust the list price or other offer terms.

Listing Agreement. The listing agreement must include the following clauses:

- ➢ **Cancellation Clause.** "Seller may cancel this Agreement prior to the ending date of the listing period without advance notice to the broker, and without payment of a commission or any other consideration, if the property is conveyed to the mortgage insurer or the mortgage holder."

- ➢ **Listing Agreement Contingency Clause.** "Sale of the property is contingent on written agreement to all sale terms by the mortgage holder and the mortgage insurer (if applicable)."

- ➢ **Property Maintenance and Expenses.** You are responsible for all property maintenance and expenses during the listing period including utilities, assessments, association dues and costs for interior and exterior upkeep required to show the property to its best advantage. Additionally, until ownership is transferred, you must report any and all property damage to us and file a hazard insurance claim for covered damage. Unless insurance proceeds are used to pay for repairs or personal property losses as provided in the mortgage documents, we may require that they be applied to reduce the mortgage debt.

- ➢ **Partial Mortgage Payments.** Beginning on _____ 1, 20___, you will be required to make partial mortgage payments of $_____ by the first day of each month during the term of the Agreement and pending transfer of property ownership. You are legally obligated to make the full amount of your current monthly mortgage payments. However, we will accept this reduced partial payment until the house is sold or this Agreement expires. The partial mortgage payments do not constitute a modification of your mortgage.

Allowable Costs that May be Deducted from Gross Sale Proceeds

. **Closing Costs.** The closing costs paid by you or on your behalf as seller must be reasonable and customary for the market. [*Choose one and delete unnecessary text.*] [Acceptable closing costs, including the commission, which may be deducted from the gross sale proceeds may not exceed $_____.] OR [Acceptable closing costs, including the commission, which may be deducted from the gross sale proceeds may not exceed ____% of the list price.] OR [Closing costs which may be deducted from the gross sale proceeds are limited to title search and escrow expenses usually paid by the seller; reasonable settlement escrow/attorney's fees; transfer taxes and recording fees usually paid by the seller; termite inspection and treatment as required by law or custom; pro-rated real property taxes; and, real estate commissions of ____ percent of the contract sales price [add other closing costs that may be included].]

Subordinate Liens. We will allow up to six percent (6%) of the unpaid principal balance of each subordinate lien in order of priority, not to exceed a total of $6,000, to be deducted from the gross sale proceeds to pay subordinate lien holders to release their liens. We require each subordinate lien holder to release you from personal liability for the loans in order for the sale to qualify for this program, but we do not take any responsibility for ensuring that the lien holders do not seek to enforce personal liability against you. Therefore, we recommend that you take steps to satisfy yourself that the subordinate lien holders release you from personal liability.

Real Estate Commissions. We will allow to be paid from sale proceeds, real estate commissions of _____ percent of the contract sales price, to be paid to the listing and selling brokers involved in the transaction. Neither you nor the buyer may receive a commission. Any commission that would otherwise be paid to you or the buyer must be reduced from the commission due on sale.

[*Optional text:*] **Please note**: We have retained a vendor to assist your listing broker with the sale. The vendor and your listing broker will work together on your behalf to facilitate the sale process.

[*Choose one and delete unnecessary text.*] (The vendor will be paid from sale proceeds [$ _____] OR [an amount equal to ____ of the sales price) OR (The vendor will be paid by us outside of the sales transaction)

Borrower Relocation Assistance. If the closing of the short sale occurs in accordance with this Agreement, you will be entitled to an incentive payment of $3,000 to assist with relocation expenses. We will instruct the settlement agent to pay you from the sale proceeds at the same time that all other payments, including the payoff of our first mortgage, are disbursed by the settlement agent. Only one payment per household is provided for the relocation assistance, regardless of the number of borrowers.

Sales Contracts. Within three business days of a bona-fide purchase offer, you must submit a Request for Approval of a Short Sale, which is attached as Exhibit A1, along with a copy of a fully executed Sales Contract, all addenda and Buyer's documentation of funds or Buyer's pre-approval or commitment letter on letterhead from a lender.

Parties to the Sale. The Sales Contract must contain the following clauses: "Seller and Buyer each represent that the sale is an "arm's length" transaction and the Seller and Buyer are unrelated to each other by family, marriage or commercial enterprise." "The Buyer agrees not to sell the property within 90 days of closing of this sale."

Closing. The closing must occur within ____ calendar days of the Sales Contract execution date.

Foreclosure Sale Suspension. We may initiate or continue the foreclosure process as permitted by the mortgage documents; however, we will suspend any foreclosure sale date until the expiration date of this Agreement or the date of closing of an approved short sale, whichever is later, provided you continue to abide by the terms and conditions of this Agreement.

.Satisfaction and Release of Liability. If all of the terms and conditions of this Agreement are met, upon sale and settlement of the property, servicer will prepare and send for recording a lien release in full satisfaction of the mortgage, foregoing all rights to personal liability or deficiency judgment.

Mortgage Insurer or Guarantor Approval. The terms and conditions of the sale are subject to the written approval of the mortgage insurer or guarantor.

Termination of this Agreement. Unless otherwise agreed by the parties, this Agreement will terminate on [*insert date*]. We may also terminate this Agreement at any time if:

➢ Your financial situation improves significantly, you qualify for loan modification, you bring the account current or you pay off the mortgage in full.

➢ You or your broker fails to act in good faith in marketing and /or closing on the sale of the property, or otherwise fails to abide by the terms of this Agreement.

➢ A significant change occurs to the property condition or value.

➢ There is evidence of fraud or misrepresentation.

- You file for bankruptcy and the Bankruptcy Court declines to approve the Agreement.

- Litigation is initiated or threatened that could affect title to the property or interfere with a valid conveyance.

- You do not make the payments required under this Agreement.

  Settlement of a Debt. The proposed transaction represents our attempt to reach a settlement of the delinquent mortgage. You are choosing to enter into this Agreement even though there is no guarantee that the transaction will be successful. In the event this transaction is unsuccessful, we may exercise our remedies under the mortgage, including foreclosure

  Acknowledgement by Listing Broker

  The undersigned listing broker ("Broker") is not a party of the Short Sale Agreement ("Agreement") above, but acknowledges that the Broker:

  Has been retained by the borrower for the sale of the property.

  Has reviewed the terms and conditions of the Agreement above.

  Agrees that in the event of a conflict between the terms of the listing agreement and the terms agreed to by the borrower in the Agreement above, the listing agreement will be deemed amended to conform to the terms of the Agreement.

  Acknowledges that pursuant to the Agreement, the Servicer will not review a sales contract unless a Request for Approval of Short Sale, attached as Exhibit A1, is completed.

Exhibit A1 – **Request for Approval of Short Sale**

[Name of Servicer] [Name of Borrower]

[Address of Servicer] [Name of Co-Borrower]

[Address of Borrower]

[Loan #]

[Servicer FAX] [Borrower Phone]

[Servicer Email] [Borrower Email]

[Date]

RE: Request for Approval of Short Sale Pursuant to Agreement Dated [Date of SSA]

This is a Request for Approval of the Short Sale Pursuant to Agreement Dated [Date of SSA] between the above referenced Servicer ("Servicer") and the borrower and co-borrower ("Borrower" or "you"). Under penalty of perjury you certify that:

1) the sale of the property is an "arm's length" transaction, between parties who are unrelated and unaffiliated by family, marriage, or commercial enterprise;

2) there are no agreements or understandings between you and the Buyer that you will remain in the property as a tenant or later obtain title or ownership of the property;

3) neither you nor the Buyer will receive any funds or commissions from the sale of the property; and

Approval to be Completed by Your Servicer

Approval of Short Sale - The Servicer consents to this Request for Approval of Short Sale and agrees to accept all net proceeds from the settlement as full and final satisfaction of the first mortgage indebtedness on the referenced property. This agreement is subject to the following:

Terms – The sale and closing comply with all terms and conditions of the Short Sale Agreement between the Servicer and the Borrower as well as all terms and representations provided herein by the Borrower.

Changes – Any change to the terms and representations contained in this Request for Approval of Short Sale or the attached sales contract between you and the buyer must be approved by the Servicer in writing. The Servicer is under no obligation to approve such changes.

Subordinate Liens – Prior to releasing any funds to holders of subordinate liens/mortgages, the closing agent must obtain a written commitment from the subordinate lien holder that it will release Borrower from all claims and liability relating to the subordinate lien in exchange for receiving the agreed upon payoff amount.

HUD-1 – A HUD-1 Settlement Statement, which will be signed by you and the buyer at closing, must be provided to the Servicer not later than one business day before the date indicated in Line 4, *Closing Date*.

Bankruptcy – If you are currently in bankruptcy or you file bankruptcy prior to closing, you must obtain any required consent or approval of the Bankruptcy Court.

Tax Consequences – A short payoff of the mortgage may have tax consequences. You are advised to contact a tax professional to determine the extent of tax liability, if any.

Credit Bureau Reporting – We will follow standard industry practice and report to the major credit reporting agencies that your mortgage was settled for less than the full payment. We have no control over or responsibility for the impact of this report on your credit score. To learn more about the potential impact of a short sale on your credit you may want to go to http://www.ftc.gov/bcp/edu/pubs/consumer/credit/cre24.shtm.

Payment Instructions – Payoff funds and a final HUD-1 Settlement Statement must be received by the Servicer within 48 hours of closing in accordance with the attached wiring instructions. [*include instructions*]

Closing Instructions – [*include proprietary closing instructions, if any*]

Disapproval To be Completed by Your Servicer

Deed in Lieu of Foreclosure

[Name of Servicer] [Name of Borrower]

[Address of Servicer] [Name of Co-Borrower]

[Address of Borrower] [Loan #]

[Servicer FAX] [Borrower Phone]

[Servicer Email] [Borrower Email]

[Date]

Dear [borrower and co-borrower name(s)]:

As your mortgage servicer, we are offering you the opportunity to participate in the federal government's **Home Affordable Foreclosure Alternatives** (HAFA) Program by utilizing the Deed-in-Lieu of Foreclosure (DIL) option to avoid foreclosure.

Home Affordable Foreclosure Alternatives Program – Deed-in-Lieu of Foreclosure

A "deed-in-lieu of foreclosure" is specifically designed to help borrowers who are unable to afford their first mortgage and want to avoid foreclosure. With a DIL, you voluntarily transfer ownership of your home and all real property secured by your mortgage loan (Property) to us to satisfy the total amount due on the first mortgage.

[Include or delete as appropriate.] While you previously entered into a Short Sale Agreement (and you complied with all your responsibilities), your Property did not sell. The DIL option will not allow you to keep your Property, however, it will prevent you from going through a foreclosure sale and it will release you from all responsibility to repay the mortgage debt. Additionally, you will be eligible to receive an assistance payment of $3,000 to help with your moving expenses.

How Does a DIL Work?

Title—You and all other occupants must vacate your Property and provide clear and marketable title with a general warranty deed or local equivalent by [*insert date at least 30 days after the date of this Agreement*].

You must also be able to deliver marketable title free of any other liens. We will contribute up to six percent (6%) of the unpaid principal balance of each subordinate lien, not to exceed a total of $6,000, toward paying off any subordinate lien holders.

We require each subordinate lien holder to release you from personal liability for the loans in order for the sale to qualify for this program, but we do not take any responsibility for ensuring that the lien holders do not seek to enforce personal liability against you. Therefore, we recommend that you take steps to satisfy yourself that the subordinate lien holders release you from personal liability.

Property Condition—You must leave the house in broom-clean condition, free of interior and exterior trash, debris or damage, and all personal belongings must be removed from the Property. The yard must be clean and neat and you must deliver all the keys and controls (e.g., garage door openers) to us.

Transfer/Closing—You may be required to sign standard pre-closing documents as well as attend a closing of the transfer of your Property where all borrowers on the mortgage must be present.

The following pages detail your responsibilities, additional information on the DIL process and the Terms and Conditions. **Additionally, this letter constitutes an agreement between us and you ("Agreement").** If you agree to the terms of the Agreement and want to proceed with a DIL, you must complete, sign and return the Agreement back to us. If you have questions, please contact us directly between the hours of [insert hours] at [insert toll free number.]

Sincerely,

[Servicer Name]

Deed In Lieu Program—Terms and Conditions

Other terms and conditions to the Deed-in-Lieu Agreement ("Agreement"):

- **Property Maintenance and Expenses.** You are responsible for all property maintenance and expenses of your Property until you convey it to us including utilities, assessments, association dues, and costs for interior and exterior maintenance. Additionally, you must report any and all property damage to us and file a hazard insurance claim for covered damage. Unless insurance proceeds are used to pay for repairs or personal property losses, we may require that they be applied to reduce the mortgage debt.

- [*Insert only if applicable:*] **Partial Mortgage Payments.** You will be required to make partial mortgage payments of $_____ by the first day of each month, beginning on _____ 1, 20___, until title to your house is transferred to us. You are legally obligated to make the full amount of your current monthly mortgage payments. However, we will accept the new partial payment until you have conveyed your Property. The partial mortgage payments do not constitute a modification of your mortgage.

- **Borrower Relocation Assistance.** If you comply with all your responsibilities under the Agreement, you will be entitled to an incentive payment of $3,000 to assist with relocation expenses. If there is a formal closing and you have vacated your Property, you will receive your incentive payment at closing. If at the time of closing you have not vacated your Property, we will mail you a check within 5 business days from when you vacate your Property and deliver the keys to us. Similarly, if a formal closing is not conducted, we will mail you a check within 5 business days from the later of when you execute the deed to us or when you vacate your Property and deliver the keys to us. Only one payment per household is provided for the relocation assistance, regardless of the number of borrowers.

- **Foreclosure Sale Suspension.** We may initiate or continue the foreclosure process as permitted by the mortgage documents; however, we will suspend any foreclosure sale date until the conveyance of your Property has been completed, provided you continue to abide by the terms and conditions of this Agreement.

- **Satisfaction and Release of Liability.** If all of the terms and conditions of this Agreement are met, upon conveyance of your Property to us by General Warranty deed or the equivalent in the state where your Property is located, we will prepare and record a lien release in full satisfaction of the mortgage, foregoing all rights to pursue a deficiency judgment.

- [*Insert only if applicable*] **Mortgage Insurer or Guarantor Approval.** The terms and conditions of the Agreement are subject to the written approval of the mortgage insurer or guarantor.

Termination of This Agreement.

We may terminate this Agreement at any time if:

- Your financial situation improves significantly, you qualify for loan modification, you bring the account current or you pay off the mortgage in full.

- You fail to act in good faith with the Agreement.

- A significant change occurs to the property condition or value.

- There is evidence of fraud or misrepresentation.

- . You file for bankruptcy and the Bankruptcy Court declines to approve the agreement.

- . Litigation is initiated or threatened that could affect title to the property or interfere with a valid conveyance.

-

- > [*Insert only if applicable:*] You do not make the payments required under this Agreement.

- > **Settlement of a Debt**. The proposed transaction represents our attempt to reach a settlement of the delinquent mortgage. You are choosing to enter into this Agreement even though there is no guarantee that the transaction will be successful. In the event this transaction is unsuccessful, we may exercise our remedies under the mortgage, including foreclosure.

- > **Possible Income Tax Considerations.** The difference between the remaining amount of principal you owe and the current market value of the property must be reported to the Internal Revenue Service (IRS) on Form 1099-C as debt forgiveness. In some cases, debt forgiveness could be taxed as income. The amount we pay you for moving expenses may also be reported as income. We suggest that you contact the IRS or your tax preparer to determine if you may have any tax liability.

- > **Credit Bureau Reporting.** We will follow standard industry practice and report to the major credit reporting agencies that your mortgage was settled for less than the full payment. We have no control over, or responsibility for the impact of this report on your credit score. To learn more about the potential impact of a deed-in-lieu on your credit, you may want to go to http://www.ftc.gov/bcp/edu/pubs/consumer/credit/cre24.shtm

- > **_DIL Program—Agreement** By signing this Agreement, you are agreeing to a deed-in-lieu of foreclosure. If you have any questions about the deed-in-lieu of foreclosure, please call us before signing and returning this Agreement.

Peggy Santmyer 214-697-5533

Join my blog. Share real estate fun and information.
Peggy's Blog

Buy Now

Buy Now

www.peggysrealestateblog.com

http://www.amazon.com/Real-Estate-Marketing-21st-Century/dp/1481112767

http://www.amazon.com/Texas-Promulgated-Real-Estate-Contracts/dp/1449913938

www.ingramcontent.com/pod-product-compliance
Lightning Source LLC
Chambersburg PA
CBHW081908170526
45167CB00007B/3201